How to Quit Smoking GOD's Way

...without using patches

and knowing GOD

loves you!

A True Personal Story by Glenn Brown

All references of the Bible are from the following: (ESV) English Standard Version, (KJV) King James Version, (NLT) New Living Translation, (ERV) Easy-to-Read Version, (GW) God's Word Translation, (NASB) New American Standard Bible, (NIV) New International Version, (NKJV) New King James Version.

How to Quit Smoking GOD's Way
By Glenn Brown
Copyright ©2012
ISBN-10:0615651267
ISBN-13:978-0-615-65126-2

Printed in the United States of America

Very Special Thanks to My Lord and My Saviour Jesus Christ who made this all possible. I would like to give thanks to my beautiful wife, Jo Ellen, whose love for me comes from GOD Himself; and also for putting the final editing on this book. I would also like to give thanks to Erica Serna who first put all my notes together for this book. Also, I would like to give thanks to my spiritual father in Christ, Mike Mooney, who has always made time for me and helped me grow in the Lord.

I dedicate this book to my Mother, Sandy T. Brown and my Dad, Leonard G. Brown and to L. G, David and Shirley Ann, whose love for me (through the years of my life) was always reaching out.

This book is designed for people who have a strong desire to quit smoking or chewing tobacco. Perhaps you have been prayed for, walked away feeling the victory, but not able to keep it and went right back into the addiction. Believe GOD and the information in this book, and you can be set free in the name of Jesus Christ!

The Great Commandment
Mark 12:28-34 (ESV)

"And one of the scribes came up and heard them disputing with one another, and seeing that He answered them well, asked Him, "Which commandment is the most important of all?" JESUS answered, "The most important is, 'Hear, O Israel: The LORD our GOD, the LORD is one. And you shall love the LORD your GOD with all your heart and with all your soul and with all your mind and with all your strength.' The second is this: 'You shall love your neighbor as yourself.' There is no other commandment greater than these." And the scribe said to Him, "You are right, Teacher. You have truly said that He is one, and there is no other besides Him. And to love Him with all the heart and with all the understanding and with all the strength, and to love one's neighbor as oneself, is much more than all whole burnt offerings and sacrifices." And when JESUS saw that he answered wisely, He said to him, "You are not far from the kingdom of GOD." And after that no one dared to ask Him any more questions."

Are you still smoking? Do you want to quit? Praise GOD! I can help and teach you how to quit, just like GOD revealed to me and released me from the chains of cigarettes.

Have you ever tried witnessing to other people about the LORD while smoking or having a wad of chew in your mouth? Or maybe you just finished smoking and smell like stale cigarettes? This used to happen to me and my heart would condemn me. Plus, the devil had a lot of ammunition to fire at me, preventing me from being an effective witness. Smoking kills our testimony. But GOD's power in us is real. We have overcome the power of the enemy by the blood of JESUS CHRIST and our testimony. To witness, we need to represent a testimony of overcoming the enemy! "And they overcame him by the blood of the Lamb, and by the word of their testimony; and they loved not their lives unto the death." **Revelation 12:11** (KJV)

We have a GOD who is Love, full of compassion, and full of patience. He knows you smoke and wants to help you quit! Believe me. He knows how to help us better than anyone, or any patch, or anything else in the world!

GOD desires for us to be like His Son, so you have to ask yourself, "What would it look like to see JESUS lighting up a cigarette and taking a puff, or putting a wad of chew in between his cheek and gum?"

> "Therefore, since we are surrounded by such a huge crowd of witnesses to the life of faith, let us strip off every weight that slows us down, especially the sin that so

easily trips us up. Let us
run with endurance the
race God has set before
us." **Hebrews 12:1** (NLT)

This verse calls us to lay aside every
weight. Smoking or chewing is an
example of the weight referred to in
the scriptures. GOD desires to lift
this weight from you! He revealed this
to me in a dream after I quit smoking.

"After this, I will pour
out My Spirit on all kinds
of people. Your sons and
daughters will prophesy,
your old men will have
dreams, and your young
men will see visions. In
those days I will pour out
My Spirit even on
servants, both men and
women. I will work
wonders in the sky and on
the earth. There will be
blood, fire, and thick

smoke. The sun will be
changed into darkness,
and the moon will be as
red as blood. Then the
great and fearful day of
the LORD will come! And
everyone who trusts in
the LORD will be saved.
There will be survivors on
Mount Zion and in
Jerusalem, just as the
LORD said. Yes, those
left alive will be the ones
the LORD has called."
Joel 2:28-32 (ERV)

In the dream, it was during the day
and I was sitting on a picnic table with
no one else around. All of the sudden
I took off flying, as I have in many
other dreams. This time, I flew
straight up and then began falling
back to earth. Do you have any idea
why? I was trying to catch a pack of
smokes! I woke up and said, "Hey
LORD, what is this about? You know I

don't smoke anymore. I don't even have the desire." He spoke to my heart saying that there are still a lot of people in the Body of CHRIST smoking. He asked me to write a book with my personal experience how He helped me to quit. The Spirit of GOD revealed to me that He would honor the book by helping anyone quit the same way He helped me. Praise the LORD!

One day I said, "LORD help me quit smoking." You know what He revealed to my spirit? "Go ahead and smoke all you want." Of course I asked astonished, "Excuse me?! What did you say?" He repeated, "Go ahead and smoke all you want."

I could not believe GOD was saying that and thought it must be the enemy. Then I heard the voice of the LORD again. He stated, "The devil did not say that. I did. It is ME. You know My voice. I said that." (The way GOD answered me, was as a thought or an impression inside of me.) By the way, I talk with GOD as if I could see Him...Remember, when we are born-again GOD lives on the inside of us.

GOD's sheep know His voice! We know His voice because He said we would! JESUS is our assurance that we can have faith in knowing His voice.

> "The gatekeeper opens
> the gate for Him, and the
> sheep recognize His voice
> and come to Him. He calls
> his own sheep by name
> and leads them out.
> After He has gathered
> His own flock, He walks
> ahead of them, and they
> follow Him because they
> know His voice. They
> won't follow a stranger;
> they will run from him
> because they don't know

his voice." **John 10:3-5** (GW)

So a couple of days went by and I was smoking like He said I could. Then, on the third day, I asked the LORD, (assuming He would say the same thing) "Hey LORD, can I have a cigarette?" But instead He responded, "No." I retorted, "Hey wait a minute. I thought You said I could smoke all I want." He questioned me "Then, why did you ask Me?" He went on to say from that moment forward, I had to ask Him whether or not I could have a cigarette. He declared that if I would be obedient to this, He would help me quit. He also told me He would remove my desire to ever want another cigarette!

I wanted to know how He would accomplish this but He said, "You are not ready for that yet, just be obedient to My voice and I will help you quit."

Please, beloved of the LORD, listen to the plea of the Spirit of GOD about this. He cares about you; He loves you! Smoking often leads to a slow and painful death, resulting in years of suffering. Emphysema slowly rots your lungs, but you are not the only one suffering. Smoking has negative effects on children around you. Cigarettes increase the risk of diseases in children such as bronchitis and even sudden infant death syndrome (SIDS). I know the addiction of smoking, but I also know the price JESUS paid on Calvary, so we can be free.

> **Isaiah 53:5** (NLT) "He was pierced because of our rebellions and crushed because of our crimes. He bore the punishment that made us whole; by His wounds we are healed."

My desire is not to judge or condemn you about smoking. I want to help you QUIT! Then GOD may receive all the Praise and Honor for helping you quit. Since we bear His name, we have the opportunity to reflect the LORD in our words and our actions. Reflecting the LORD reveals the deep love of GOD to a cold and lost world.

It is time that we, the Body of CHRIST, WAKE UP! We must do what we know is right because the coming of our LORD JESUS CHRIST is at hand. We will be without spot and wrinkle before Him at His coming. "CHRIST died so that He could give the church to Himself like a bride in all her beauty. He died so that the church could be holy and without fault, with no evil or sin or any other thing wrong in it." **Ephesians 5:27** (ERV)

> "We have all these great people around us as

examples. Their lives tell
us what faith means. So
we, too, should run the
race that is before us
and never quit. We
should remove from our
lives anything that would
slow us down and the sin
that so often makes us
fall. We must never stop
looking to JESUS. He is
the leader of our faith,
and He is the one who
makes our faith
complete. He suffered
death on a cross. But He
accepted the shame of
the cross as if it were
nothing because of the
joy He could see waiting
for Him. And now He is
sitting at the right side
of GOD's throne. Think
about JESUS. He
patiently endured the

angry insults that sinful
people were shouting at
Him. Think about Him so
that you won't get
discouraged and stop
trying. You are
struggling against sin, but
you have not had to give
up your life for the
cause. You are children
of GOD, and He speaks
words of comfort to you.
You have forgotten these
words:

"My child, don't think the
LORD's discipline is
worth nothing, and don't
stop trying when He
corrects you. The LORD
disciplines everyone He
loves; He punishes
everyone He accepts as a
child."

So accept sufferings like a father's discipline. GOD does these things to you like a father correcting his children. You know that all children are disciplined by their fathers. So, if you never receive the discipline that every child must have, you are not true children and don't really belong to GOD. We have all had fathers here on earth who corrected us with discipline. And we respected them. So it is even more important that we accept discipline from the Father of our spirits. If we do this, we will have life. Our fathers on earth disciplined us for a short time in the way they thought was best. But GOD disciplines us to help us so that we can be holy like Him. We don't enjoy discipline when we get it. It is painful. But later, after we have learned our lesson from it, we will enjoy the peace that comes from doing what is right.

 You have become weak, so make yourselves strong again. Live in the right way so that you will be saved and your weakness will not cause you to be lost.

 Try to live in peace with everyone. And try to keep your lives free from sin. Anyone whose life is not holy will never see the LORD." **Hebrews 12:1-14** (ERV)

The way the LORD helped me to never desire another cigarette again was through a very disturbing dream. I asked the Holy Spirit the meaning of the dream. He responded, "Every time you smoke a cigarette, you are committing adultery straight against GOD."

> **2 Corinthians 6:16-7:1**
> "GOD's temple cannot have anything to do with idols, and we are the temple of the living GOD. As GOD said, "I will live with them and walk with them; I will be their GOD, and they will be my people." "So come away from those people and separate yourselves from them, says the LORD. Don't touch anything that

is not clean, and I will accept you." "I will be your father, and you will be My sons and daughters, says the LORD All-Powerful." Dear friends, we have these promises from GOD. So we should make ourselves pure—free from anything that makes our body or our soul unclean. Our respect for GOD should make us try to be completely holy in the way we live."

The dream worked! I've never looked at another cigarette the same. They became filthy to me. I grabbed the pack of smokes on my table then threw them back down as fast as I could. I would like to say I quit that night, but I didn't because of the addiction.

I finally did quit just one week after that. I couldn't take it anymore. Every time I would smoke, I remembered what the Holy Spirit said. I would become overwhelmed with conviction, 46 years old, a cigarette in hand, crying my heart out.

My last pack was Saturday at work in Charlotte, North Carolina. I promised GOD numerous times that I would not buy another pack, yet always broke down and bought one. This time I knew it was different because of the dream the LORD had given me about adultery towards GOD.

At the time I was working on heavy equipment (newspaper presses). I was helping on the installation, the final stages. While fine tuning the press we ran into an electrical problem. This particular day was the electrician's day off. I was staying at the same hotel as the electrician, so I gave him a call and told him the problem. We decided the best thing was for him to come to work and check it out. He didn't drive so I told him I would pick him up.

While preparing to leave, the LORD said "Glenn, leave your pack of cigarettes here." I replied, "LORD, I won't smoke on the way there." This conversation went on and on. He continued suggesting and I kept saying the same thing. Then I could feel Him and as if there were tears in His eyes, He said "Do you love Me?" I would like to say I left the pack, but I didn't. I got in the van, with the cigarettes, to pick up the electrician.

I didn't get very far before I started smoking. I attempted to ignore my conscience, but it wasn't working this time. Then I heard the LORD say very sternly, "Put the cigarette out." I insisted, "It's only halfway." He said, "Put it out!!" Then I was looking at the cigarette trying to decide what to do.

He asked a second time, "Glenn, do you love Me?" I didn't hesitate, I love the LORD. I threw the cigarette out. I still had almost a full pack with me, but the Holy Spirit reminded me about the dream and that it was time to quit.

Then the LORD said, "Now, throw out that pack, Glenn." I said, "LORD, that's a full pack. I just bought them. There are only 3 missing." He told me again to throw the pack out. I didn't right away. I had a thought that if I threw them out, I'd be littering. But I regained perspective and realized I was in the middle of a breakthrough in the addiction. Please, understand I care about our environment, but why would I be thinking about not littering at this particular moment when GOD Almighty is helping me quit smoking.

 I knew I was on the verge of a breakthrough because the enemy, who doesn't care about you or me, showed up to destroy my progress. JESUS said it like this in **John 10:10** (NASB), "The thief does not come except to steal, and to kill, and to destroy. I have come that they may have life, and that they may have it more abundantly." Beloved, smoking steals our wind to run or walk, smoking kills our breath and our ability to smell, smoking destroys our lungs. The enemy wants to steal the very life GOD gave us. Listen to the Words of JESUS, "Do you love Me?" He will help you same way He helped me. All thanks and glory be to GOD because I do not smoke anymore!

Ask the LORD to help you quit. He will, just like He helped me. Also brothers and sisters of mine in the LORD, I love you. Just ask Him to help you quit, He will help you! Be obedient to the Holy Spirit's leading, (which will be like nudges or impressions upon your thoughts) and you will grow to know Him on a more personal level.

> **Romans 8:14** (ESV) "For all who are led by the Spirit of GOD are sons of GOD."

> "But when He, the Spirit of truth, comes, He will guide you into all the truth; for He will not speak on His own initiative, but whatever He hears, He will speak; and He will disclose to you what is to come." **John 16:13** (NIV)

During the process of being led by the Spirit of GOD, you will start to notice how you start to cut back, give GOD the praise! Let me encourage you to keep going. Do not give up on this, because this will take time. Always, always ask the Holy Spirit to help you, not only in quitting smoking or chewing, but in everything you do.

Read and meditate on **John 15:1-14** (NLT)

> "I am the true grapevine, and my Father is the gardener. He cuts off every branch of mine that doesn't produce fruit, and He prunes the branches that do bear fruit so they will produce even more. You have already been pruned and purified by the message I have given you. Remain in Me, and I will remain in you. For a branch cannot produce fruit if it is severed from the vine, and you cannot be fruitful unless you remain in Me.

Yes, I am the vine; you are the branches. Those who remain in Me, and I in them, will produce much fruit. For apart from Me you can do nothing. Anyone who does not remain in Me is thrown away like a useless branch and withers. Such branches are gathered into a pile to be burned. But if you remain in Me and My words remain in you, you may ask for anything you want, and it will be granted! When you produce much fruit, you are My true disciples. This brings great glory to my Father.

I have loved you even as the Father has loved Me.

Remain in My love. When
you obey My
commandments, you
remain in My love, just as
I obey my Father's
commandments and
remain in His love. I have
told you these things so
that you will be filled
with My joy. Yes, your
joy will overflow! This is
My commandment: Love
each other in the same
way I have loved you.
There is no greater love
than to lay down one's
life for one's friends. You
are My friends if you do
what I command."

Now, there will come a time during
this process that the Holy Spirit will
start to impress on you not to smoke
at all. Sometimes you will go hours
without having or wanting a cigarette.

Or maybe you will go a whole night or day. Please, beloved, respond to the Holy Spirit's nudges about this, because this is the same way He helped me quit smoking.

Also beloved, I want you to know this: That during this process of quitting, I kept a daily relationship with the LORD JESUS through reading Scripture. Every day! This is very important. This is number one, no matter what. "But seek first the kingdom of GOD and His righteousness, and all these things shall be added to you." **Matthew 6:33** (NKJV)

Worshipping GOD provides the strength to quit. For me, worship is getting lost in His presence, getting to a place where nothing else matters. Worship daily. Turn on Christian radio or put in a worship CD. Sing to the LORD with songs of Praise and Worship, at least three songs or more a day. Rest in GOD's presence, which for me means to simply enjoy being in His manifested presence. Then as you sing to Him, meditate on who He is…You can also worship through reading Scripture.

Meditate on **Psalm 100** (KJV)

> "Make a joyful noise unto the LORD, all ye lands. Serve the LORD with gladness: come before His presence with singing. Know ye that the LORD He is GOD: it is He that hath made us, and not we ourselves; we are His people, and the sheep of His pasture. Enter into His gates with thanksgiving, and into His courts with praise: be thankful unto Him, and bless His name. For the LORD is good; His mercy

is everlasting; and His
truth endureth to all
generations."

Learn what it means to worship Him.
The Word says, "You make the path of
life known to me. Complete joy is in
Your presence. Pleasures are by Your
side forever." **Psalm 16:11** (GW)
Stay in His presence as long as you
can. This helped me a lot, because
**BEING IN GOD'S PRESENCE
HELPED KILL THE DESIRE TO
SMOKE**. Do you really want to quit?
Then, Worship Him instead of
smoking.

FAITH CONFESSIONS

When JESUS was tempted in the
desert, He used Scripture to declare
truth and holiness. Here are some
Scriptures that you can use as
powerful faith confessions, resisting
temptation and declaring truth.

Philippians 4:13 (KJV) "I can do all things through CHRIST who strengtheneth me."

Colossians 1:13-14 (ERV) "GOD made us free from the power of darkness. And He brought us into the kingdom of His dear Son. The Son paid the price to make us free. In Him we have forgiveness of our sins."

2 Corinthians 7:1 (ERV) "Dear friends, we have these promises from GOD. So we should make ourselves pure—free from anything that makes our body or our soul unclean. Our respect for GOD should make us

try to be completely holy
in the way we live."

Romans 6:13 (NLT) "Do
not let any part of your
body become an
instrument of evil to
serve sin. Instead, give
yourselves completely to
GOD, for you were dead,
but now you have new
life. So use your whole
body as an instrument to
do what is right for the
glory of GOD."

Romans 12:1-2 (ERV)
"So I beg you, brothers
and sisters, because of
the great mercy GOD has
shown us, offer your lives
as a living sacrifice to
Him—an offering that is
only for GOD and
pleasing to Him.

Considering what He has done, it is only right that you should worship Him in this way. Don't change yourselves to be like the people of this world, but let GOD change you inside with a new way of thinking. Then you will be able to understand and accept what GOD wants for you. You will be able to know what is good and pleasing to Him and what is perfect."

I also believe you can apply these same principles to any tobacco product. Thanks be unto GOD that you are taking the time to read my book. GOD sees the desire in your heart to quit, and I believe that GOD will help you, and lead you to never smoke again!

If you are far from GOD or have never asked Him to forgive you of your sins, let us pray together, (read this out-loud) "Heavenly Father, forgive me of my sins and cleanse me from all unrighteousness. LORD JESUS, I ask You to come into my heart, so that I can be born-again. I believe in my heart that GOD raised JESUS CHRIST from the dead. JESUS, I now confess You as my LORD and Saviour. I am saved. Father, Thank You that You care so deeply about me and Thank You for Your amazing unconditional Love. I ask You to help me quit smoking the same way you helped Brother Glenn. In the mighty name of JESUS CHRIST of Nazareth, Amen.

www.ingramcontent.com/pod-product-compliance
Lightning Source LLC
Chambersburg PA
CBHW071116090426
42737CB00013B/2598